Singapore
IN FOCUS

TEXT BY SIMON BARNES
PHOTOGRAPHED BY ALAIN EVRARD

Singapore — an overgrown mudflat
that became the great crossroads of
Asia.

D1228053

CFW GUIDEBOOKS
Hong Kong

An island surrounded and crosscut by water, Singapore exists because of water. An English gentleman and visionary saw the uninviting flatlands in 1819 and imagined a trading post for the British East India Company. It took some imagining. He found a coastline littered with human skulls, detritus of a history of piratical battles, on an island named after a lion once spotted in the jungles there. The lion was thought to be a good omen — Singa Pura means Lion City. The city was a mewling kitten when Sir Thomas Stamford Raffles first set

eyes on it; today it roars, though it does its roaring in a highly civilised fashion.

And today's Singapore is a hard city to learn. Antiseptic and soulless, claim some short-stay travellers who saw only the swingeing fines for litterbugs and jaywalkers and the draconian rulings on traffic flow, failing to notice the odd contrasts between clean concrete towers and crumbling street corners, buildings with the sad smell of brick that has stood for years in tropical rainstorms and has absorbed the damp into its soul. The crossroads city of Singapore is at a crossroads of history, caught between its go-getting future of taut organisation, and its leisurely, more anarchic past.

MARKET STREET

The *becha* is a part of life in many Asian cities, the best form of public transport available. It was part of old Singapore. In new Singapore it is dying out, slow and inefficient and blocking the flow of the island's traffic — a heinous crime in today's hustling city. The tough measures taken to keep the traffic moving through the commercial district even at peak hours display the kind of awesome practicality that sums up the organisation of modern Singapore. Cars must pay crippling tolls to enter certain areas at peak times unless they carry a full load of passengers. Singapore works hard, and it starts work on time. Cogs mesh, Singapore *works*.

It is not that Singapore, like that other seaborn city of the East, Hong Kong, revels in destruction of the old and in newness for its own sake. It is just that everything must first pass the test of practicality. Take the padang: the greatest prime site in Singapore, a vacant lot in the heart of town. It serves a purpose: people play games there. Cricket, hockey, football. It is more than a green lung in the midst of the city traffic, it is a great recreation area.

And it is also a marvellous public relations statement: the green acres of people at play make plain the message: Singapore is for the Singaporeans first and for business and foreign investment second.

Singapore is undisputably a Chinese town. Raffles invited merchants from every trading station in Asia to come and compete here, but the Chinese won easily. They are better at it than anyone else. Today, seventy six per cent of Singaporeans are Chinese. Malaysia is just a few minutes drive away, a short haul across the causeway. Only fourteen per cent of Singaporeans are Malay. The Upper Serangoon Road, though, might be a street in an Indian town. A nice street, that is, in a nice town. Life is lived out on the streets here, and the food, stingingly hot, splashed from silver pails onto banana leaves and eaten with the fingers, is unmatchable.

This is a young city. More than half the people are under twenty. There are many different races and cultures here, and even among the Chinese there are many different dialects spoken. A Chinese from the north will find a southern dialect incomprehensible. There is little crossover. It is not too wild a generalisation to call each of the youngsters of any race a patriot. But his loyalty is to Singapore.

There are times here when it is hard to believe you are in Asia among the *Coca-cola,* the bowling alleys, the sporty week-ends. Perhaps the only thing missing is the cynicism about Western-style entertainments and ways of life, an attitude that is *de rigueur* among the gildered children of the West. Singapore is a city that is founded on optimism. How else could it have begun, and once begun, survive? This optimism, this utter belief in the future of Singapore, is a characteristic shared by Raffles and by Singapore's strong-man Prime Minister, Lee Kwan Yew. The youth of the city have picked up on this.

There is a naivete about the place and about the hard-working ambitious youth who work and play with such rigorous compartmentalisation, that is at the same time endearingly attractive and desperately irritating. It is hard to penetrate this layer of sincerity, because this layer is, in fact, heart deep. So many of the young Singaporeans one meets are genuinely hard-working, devoted to family, ambition, and to the town where they live, that one ends up half-infected and half convinced by their brave new world enthusiasm.

Cynicism, or realism as the West prefers to call it, is seen as a rather decadent and slightly indecent item of Western luxury that one would rather do without. The kids here are too anxious for hi-fi and kids of their own (two is enough, though, Lee Kwan Yew points out) to be bothered with doubting the vitality of their lives. Only from the dizzy heights of success or failure can such assessments in fact be made: in Singapore the quest for success dominates thinking.

This is a young place, anxious to

learn, anxious to please, anxious to
succeed. Hong Kong feels to the
visitor like a rather gaudily dressed
hustler looking for a fast buck:
Singapore is more like a brilliantly
promising recruit in a big firm: sober-
suited, short-haired, hard-working,
and filled with a boundless
determination to make it to the top.

SWIMMING LAGOON
CAMP SITE
RESTAURANT

ROLLER SKATING RINK

ERRY TERMINAL

CYCLE KIOSK

ABLE CAR STATION

RRENDER CHAMBER
STAURANT

RT SILOSO

Singapore is wholly without the precocious world-weariness of Western kids. Youths here are cleaner than clean, super sporty, hard working, burger chomping, gleaming with health, nurturing the secret vice of massive drinking. Of soft drinks. As for drugs — why? The very thought appals.

In such a clean and organised community, the extraordinary has to be staged. This is not one of your spontaneous towns living up the "teeming streets of the East" cliché. The Dragon Boat Festival is heavily backed, sponsored, and officially promoted. Tourists love it. So, incidentally, do Singaporeans.

Singapore has broken all the rules for Asian cities. According to continent-wide, time-honoured practice, Asian cities are filthy, traffic-clogged places where nothing grows except babies. Singapore used to be conformist. Then the government announced that they would turn Singapore into a garden city. Old Singapore hands fell off their chairs laughing at the utter ludicrousness of the proposal. No one is laughing now. Today's Singapore is the only clean, green, freely moving city in Asia. To create such an environment is more miraculous than any of the economic marvels of the post-colonial age.

For we all know about the "economic miracle" side of modern Singapore, there are plenty of other economic miracles to be found among emerging nations. What is remarkable is that Singapore has come to terms with its colonial past, as a logical part in the history that has brought today's city into existence. Old colonial buildings are used by the government without a shred of apology; the statue of Raffles has not been destroyed, nor his name purged from history books. The reality of Singapore's achievements has forestalled the need for post-colonial paranoia. For Singapore is literally unrecognisable from the city it was 10 years ago. So is the distant neighbour Hong Kong, with which Singapore is so regularly compared; Hong Kong with its motto of pull down the old, invest in the new. Singapore has plenty of new buildings, but it has kept many of the old. The mania for destruction has passed it by. The place is more restful, more permanent in feeling, more secure than Hong Kong. In Singapore, the main change is in tone: cleanliness and order. The price of this change is high, especially if you get caught littering and face the fine. But the clean blending of old and new makes the city something different: unlike Hong Kong, Singapore is a city carefully thought out as a place for human beings to live in.

The Singapore Tourist Promotion Board puts on a daily cultural show for tourists. It is interesting to speculate whether the show's title is intentionally ironic, but in its way it could serve as a motto for the traveller in Singapore — traces of the old ways of a dozen and more Asian communities can be found, and viewed, in the comfort of a modern, clean, green city. "Instant Asia." Only five dollars.

This all goes to make crossroads-city Singapore a cultural schizophrenic — hamming it up for the tourists, involved in the mainstream of Western culture and, at the same time, deeply and irrefragably Asian. And Asians do not throw family and tradition out of the window in a hurry.

Freedom of action is not an attainable commodity in Singapore. From littering upward, life is organised, ruled, watched. Brilliantly organised media saturation campaigns reach everyone. But the Asian spirit seems able to tolerate what a Westerner might find impossible — for here, freedom of spirit and of worship is absolute.

Singapore is a crazy mixed stew of the great religions of the world. The main religions are Buddhism, Islam, Christianity, Hinduism and Taoism, but there is a spicey undertone of more exotic creeds. There are Sikhs, Jains, Jews and even Zoroastrians.

The great clashes and crossovers of cosmologies, beliefs and ethical systems puts one in mind of the Buddhist monk who was shown a bible. The Sermon on the Mount was read to him, the monk listening, nodding his head with quiet agreement. The reading ended, the monk smiled. "That man was close to Buddhahood," he remarked.

But throughout the cosmic patchwork of Singapore's religious life, it is the Chinese patterns that dominate — the ancient rituals for coping with life and death. Among the older people, the old ways of luck and hope remain unquestioned. Once the walker has stepped away from the tree-lined, skyscraper-shaded boulevards and into the older parts of town, the sweet stench of incense becomes a *leitmotiv* — a constant mnemonic of the fact that one is in a Chinese town.

I think one of the reasons why Chinese religious practices are so refreshing and relaxing to the observing Westerner is that the whole system and practice appear utterly beyond the bounds of possible comprehension. It seems that lighting joss in the temple is at the same time an expression of deep commitment and faith in the eternal patterns, and an item of almost routine superstition, on a par with trying to run downstairs before the flush stops.

An old English story makes plain the attitude many people perhaps have to the ways of seeking luck and insuring against evil fates. A wrinkle-faced farmer was asked why he still put out small offerings to the fairies. Did he really believe in fairies? He wouldn't say he *believed* in them, no.

Then why did he bother to leave them gifts?

He considered the question. "Because," he said eventually, "I'd be a bloody fool if I didn't."

It is easy to misunderstand the Chinese fascination with, and almost reverence for, death. The Western understanding of "ancestor worship" is the coarsest of misinterpretations. It is not death that is central, but the constant unchanging patterns of life. Ancestors are no more worshipped than an eldest son. It is a question of respect for the past, for it has given you today, and hope for the future. Death is seen in the content of life and as such, can be lived with.

Singapore quickly dispels the "inscrutable oriental" myth. A Chinese architect, designer of one of Asia's great modern hotels, once defined good taste as "the opposite of a Chinese restaurant." If bad taste is noise, exuberance, garish colours, explosive gaiety and grinning fellowship, then Singapore at Chinese New Year exhibits the most execrable taste in the world.

The West has lost many of its rituals. There are no longer clearly fixed patterns for dealing with the routine emergencies of mourning and celebration. It is hard to know the correct way to behave at a birthday or a funeral. The West has even lost a comprehensible Christmas.

The East, and perhaps the Chinese in particular, appear to have more pertinacity than that. The fizzing rituals of family life over the new year are not relinquished, despite the fact that fizzy Coca-cola is sold down the road. To live in a Chinese community over new year is to know a deep feeling of envy; envy of that certainty of the continuity of life and its patterns that flow through each year as the tide flows through a fisherman's day.

But it is not a question of spontaneity. There is a proper time or work, and a proper time to go crazy. A man must be properly sober and responsible, but he needs a time when he is allowed to cut loose. That is what festivals are all about. Singapore is full of them. Every religion has its high days, and with such a plethora of religions, there is a positive glut of festivals.

The Chinese must take the prize for the noisiest religious practices in the world. Any Lion Dance accompaniment sounds like the rhythmic collapse of a pyramid of saucepans; while the Chingay festival, a parade of bands, cymbals, pugilists and prancing lion dancers, simply surpasses belief.

A Catholic of rather ascetic sensibilities once made a rather revealing remark, revealing truths both about himself and the on the subject under discussion. He declared: "But the Chinese religious festivals are so vulgar."

He is absolutely right, of course, but he had forgotten his classical education, forgotten that to be vulgar means to belong to the people. Not the elite, and not the fools: everyone. Now, Catholicism has its festival moments of wild vulgarity, and at the same time affords deep solace to the most astringent of intellectuals.

I have never heard anyone attempt an intellectual justification of Chinese festival and ritual, not, I suspect, because such a justification would be beyond the wit of man, but because it would never occur to a Chinese that a festival required justification. Of

course it's good — it happens every year, doesn't it?

And Singapore's year is a year of festivals. Christmas and Easter. The fasting month of Ramadan, when the Moslems must forego all food, drink and smokes in the daylight hours, which is concluded by the Hari Raya shindig of rejoicing. In November, Deepavali, the Festival of Lights, is celebrated by the Hindus, to commemorate the slaying of the mythical tyrant king Naragusura by the wondrous Lord Krishna: the triumph of light over darkness. Buddhists honour the birth, death and

enlightenment of the Lord Buddha on Vesak Day.

As for the Chinese, they clean their homes, pay their debts, buy a new suit of clothes and have a good haircut, because new year is the time for fresh starts, and for recollecting and honouring the old ties of family. In some places new year is a time also of a million firecrackers, but in Singapore this is banned, as one might have guessed. In the summer, the Festival of the Hungry Ghosts is celebrated: the souls of the dead have been released to roam the earth: joss is burned every where and food is offered as appeasement. Perhaps the most delightful festival occurs in the autumn when families, the children carrying paper lanterns, set out to admire the full moon and to feast, lit by the flickering candles and the heady light of the moon, on the rich and powerful stuff of moon cakes.

The most disturbing festival in Singapore is the Indian day of Thaipusam. Devotees of the Hindu god Lord Subramaniom do penance by struggling from the Perumal Temple in Serangoon Road to the Chettiar Temple in Tank Road, hideously perforated with skewers. This extreme observance of the penitential festival is no longer much performed in India itself, oddly enough, but in civilised Singapore, and in Malaysia it still goes on in an agony of devotion.

The mutation of Singapore into today's boomtown has been so complete it is hard to remember that, for all practical purposes, the place has existed for just the blinking of an historical eye. The last tiger of Singapore was shot in 1931.

Night falls, work is over, and the Singaporeans go out to seek their pleasures. The British colonials of the past used to wait for the sun to go down before they permitted themselves the first supremely gratifying drink of the tropical day. But Singaporeans think of just one thing once the street lamps are lit.

No race treats the whole matter of food with the single-minded dedication of the Chinese. The Middle Eastern masters look decadent, and the French artists appear downright frivolous, when compared with the reverential gourmandising gourmets of Asia.

Do the Chinese eat to live or live to
eat? The distinction is meaningless.
Food is life, and therefore to be
celebrated. And there are more
different cuisines than there are
religions in Singapore: international
hotel food, the regional styles of
China from the blandness of the
Cantonese to the electric spice of
Szechuan ... the street stalls are part
of Singapore life, and woe betide
any stall-holder with the slightest
hint of dirt. The health inspectors
will have his guts for *dim sum*.
Singaporeans and visitors can gorge
with a quiet mind.

For the visitor especially, Singapore
is an unbroken succession of eating
treats. The boast of Singapore's
tourist promoters is also, probably, an
accurate statement: that the food here
is the best in Asia. No matter what
kind of food you are talking about.
For example a Brahmin friend assures
me that the best Indian food in the
world, better even than the food to be
found in India itself, is to be found in
the Upper Serangoon Road. I have
never had a better meal any where
else in the world, in fact, and it cost
me just a couple of Singapore dollars.

For fair price, cleanliness and
above all, quality, Singapore has got
to be unmatchable. Eating out at the
stalls, spearing fizzing hot spiced
noodles and drinking from a glass full
of Anchor beer that is misty with
condensation, is one of the great
experiences of Asian eating: there is
plenty of fancy stuff to choose from
too.

Singaporean cooks have never been
narrow-minded. Surrounded by
culinary influences from all over Asia,
to borrow a little cooking lore and to

adapt it to your own style was part of an inevitable process. For example the southern Chinese dishes, traditionally bland to the point, to many palates, of being downright dull, has fallen under the Malay fondness for mild spices. The hybrid is known as nonya food. Even the traditional Chinese styles of cooking have not escaped the process of borrowing and experiment. The Singaporeans love food, love the whole process of eating, eating out: celebration.

Singapore bans the sale of *Playboy* and the nightlife is nothing like the wild excesses of Bangkok and Manila. Rather, there is charm. The darker side of the night can be found in Singapore, but it takes some finding.

But Singapore does not go straight to bed after supper. The young people get drunk on *7-up* and go boogying like Western kids, while the visitor can find more ancient joys as he looks for culture — the culture that the go-getting, going-places youngsters of Singapore seem on the verge of losing.

The great anomaly of Singapore is Bugis Street: in this super-clean city people like the one on the left flirt with customers out for a good time. It's a boy, of course, one of the famed epicene beauties of Bugis. Why did Bugis Street remain untouched, unchanged for so long, with its shutter-clicking tourists and its hustling transvestites? It was a glaring inconsistency, but it is being "cleaned up" now. Many may mourn its passing; an imperfection that makes you realise that Singapore is only human. I fancy few Singaporeans will show much sorrow at seeing the place go. They aim to go on going places. They've got *work* to do...